CONTENTS

The Tale of Seven Pillars

Surviving Startup to Becoming the Giant

WORKBOOK

Published in the United States of America
ISBN 978-0-9898427-6-1 Champion Publishing Inc

PILLAR 1 ~ YOU MUST HAVE THE QUALITIES OF A HIGH ACHIEVER

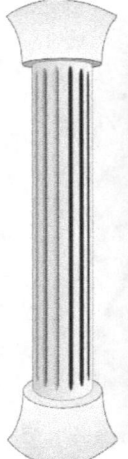
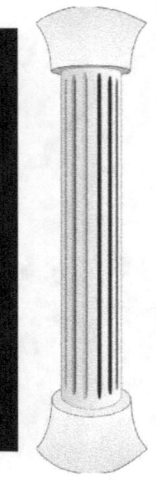

The first rule of successful business is that you—the business owner—must be qualified to start and operate a business. You may have picked up this book because you've always dreamed of owning your own business, but you're not really sure you have what it takes. The lessons in this section will help you learn about all the skills, personality traits, and habits that should help you be a successful business owner. They will also show you the harsh reality of starting up a business. If it's not what you expected, I'm happy to have saved you the time, money, and heartache by learning these lessons now.

Characteristics Of Those With High Probability Of Failure

We don't like to talk about failure, but it is a realistic possibility for anyone who attempts something new. Thomas Edison was unsuccessful in his first 99 attempts to invent the light bulb. You and I should be grateful he didn't give up! Failure doesn't mean you'll never be successful. Great lessons can be learned through the things we try that don't work.

Most businesses fail because of one or two weaknesses within the business owner. Below is a list of some of the personal characteristics that can lead to business failure. Mark the ones that are a concern to you.

- ☐ Lack of clarity and focus
- ☐ Lack of ambition
- ☐ Lack of persistence
- ☐ Negativity
- ☐ Lack of knowledge
- ☐ Lack of spending control/poor money management
- ☐ Lack of enthusiasm
- ☐ Lack of flexibility

- ☐ Does not work well with others
- ☐ Lack of self-discipline
- ☐ Lack of leadership
- ☐ Dishonesty
- ☐ Lack of planning
- ☐ Indecisiveness
- ☐ Lack of capital
- ☐ Ego

What is your plan for addressing these personal weaknesses? _____

_____

_____

_____

Define Your Own Success Standard

What would success look like to you personally? This is not the same as your vision statement that defines what success looks like for the company. Before you start this start-up journey, define success for you personally. It is hard to know when you have reached the finish line if you do not know where it is.

> Before you start this start-up journey, define success for you personally. It is hard to know when you have reached the finish line if you do not know where it is.

What is your definition of success? _____

_____

_____

_____

How will you measure success in your business? _____

_____

_____

_____

Earlier, you identified your estimated earnings for the first year of business. Other than money, what are you looking for in this business? _____

_____

_____

_____

Some people say that a business will be successful to the degree that it finds ways to give back to its community or meaningful causes. What are some partnerships you can develop so you can give back? How will this make you successful? _____

_____

_____

_____

What do you expect a workweek to be like? When will you have down time and time for your family and other responsibilities? _____

_____

_____

_____

Great People Skills Can Make The Difference

We all have met people with great people skills and others with terrible people skills. What specific characteristics are you looking for in a person with great people skills? _____

_____

_____

_____

List on the lines below five top characteristics identified above. Rate yourself in each skill.

	poor	average	excellent
_____	|-------------------|	-------------------|
_____	|-------------------|	-------------------|
_____	|-------------------|	-------------------|
_____	|-------------------|	-------------------|
_____	|-------------------|	-------------------|

How effective are your listening skills? Below are some helpful tips for improving your listening skills.

1. **Give the speaker undivided attention.** Repeat his or her words in your head as you hear them.
2. **Allow your nonverbal behavior to communicate that you are listening.** Nod in agreement, smile, say, "yes" or "good point."
3. **Provide immediate feedback.** Recognize that your personal opinions or perceptions can cloud the words others speak. Say, "What I heard you say was…" or summarize what you heard.
4. **Delay judgment.** Don't interrupt. Wait until the speaker is finished before expressing any disagreement or concerns. Give the same grace you expect to receive.
5. **Respond with kindness, even if you disagree.** Express your opinion without using condescending language.

Which of the suggestions above do you need to incorporate into your listening skills?

_____

_____

_____

You May Be A Team Of One

In a start-up business, you will have many people that I call "must hires." You hire them because you need them to perform certain tasks. There is no guarantee that you will ever have a personal relationship with them. You shouldn't expect to, in fact.

Your business might be one you can operate alone. However, you might need to hire people to perform specific tasks. Almost every business manual written warns about the dangers of making the wrong hire. These most often include family members or friends.

Why is it unwise to hire family members or friends to work in your business? _____

_____

_____

_____

Excel At The Right Business

Success in one area does not necessarily produce success in other areas. Though some business principles are transferrable, some leadership skills are not. Take a close look at your personality type. Why do you think you are qualified to lead this business? _____

_____

_____

_____

_____

_____

How can your prior success help you be successful in this business? _____

_____

_____

_____

_____

_____

_____

The hard truth is that your personal experience can only take your idea so far. Just because I am a successful business owner doesn't mean I can be successful at owning any type of business. Whether you think you know the industry or you already have a plan, you may have overestimated the demand or profitability for your good or service. We sometimes forget that billionaire Donald Trump once tried his hand at owning an airline.

> The hard truth is that your personal experience can only take your idea so far.

Are You An Effective Time And Priority Manager?

How you manage your time is critical to your success in life and business. According to statistics, every year the average American invests…

- 106 days sleeping

- 87 days working

- 16 days online

- 12 days commuting

- 45 days watching television

There are very few skills more beneficial to master in business, than time and priority management.

That's a total of 256 days invested in these five activities. In other words, 73% of the year is spent before the year begins. Everything else in life must be squeezed into 99 days!

There are very few skills more beneficial to master in business, than time and priority management. The ability to start each day knowing what must be done, and the discipline to do it, is a personality trait that the successful have mastered.

When was the last time you analyzed the way you spend your time? Use this diagram to evaluate your daily schedule. Each wedge represents an hour. Be sure to account for the five activities above along with activities that are unique to you.

How you manage your time reveals your priorities. Based on the allocation of your time, what are your priorities (in order of most to least time allotted)?

_____

_____

_____

Do you think your priorities consistent with those of successful entrepreneurs? Explain. ___

_____

_____

What are some things you need to eliminate from your schedule so you can focus on your business? _____

_____

_____

What are some things you need to add to your schedule so you can be more effective at running your business? _____

_____

_____

Are You An "Industry Expert?"

Will you know your industry better than anyone who works for you? Will you have an area within your industry that you will know better than anyone else? Seek to be an expert in something within your business. Customers and employees can tell when you have no idea what is going on. The good news is that they can also tell when you have a keen understanding of an area as well.

The dictionary defines an expert as *a person who has special skill or knowledge in some particular field*. There is no special training necessary. Becoming an expert is as simple as

If you read two books on a specific subject, you would know more than 95% of everyone else.

reading three books on a topic about which you are passionate. I recently learned that if you read two books on a specific subject, you would know more than 95% of everyone else. Continue to learn, whether from reading books, going to trade association conferences, or training seminars.

What are some subjects about which you might be considered an expert?

1. _____

2. _____

3. _____

How can you increase your knowledge level of the industry your company will serve? _____

_____

_____

_____

Are You A Self-Starter?

One of the great things about being an entrepreneur is the freedom to do things on your own. One of the scariest things about being an entrepreneur is the freedom to do things on your own. The thrill and stress are two sides of the same coin.

Describe a time when you started or helped start something. _____

_____

_____

_____

What are three things you learned about yourself in the process described above?

1. _____

2. _____

3. _____

How will the lessons listed above help you be more successful in business? _____

_____

_____

_____

What is your plan for dealing with the obstacles and frustration that are common while starting up a business? Mark this response so you can find it when the need arises. _____

_____

_____

_____

How would you describe your self-initiative?

☐ I'm not much of a go-getter.
☐ I have a lot of ideas but struggle to complete them.
☐ I have no problem starting and finishing.

How Strong Is Your Success Instinct?

> If your success instinct isn't very strong, be aware that this might be a limiting factor.

The dictionary defines instinct as *a natural or innate impulse, inclination, or tendency*. People who have a strong success instinct face the same obstacles and challenges as everyone else. They just power through them because of their strong success instinct.

If your success instinct isn't very strong, be aware that this might be a limiting factor. You should be prepared to deal with the obstacles that have the ability to stop you in your tracks. This is different from being pessimistic. Pessimists seldom succeed as entrepreneurs because they convince themselves that success isn't possible.

> Pessimists seldom succeed as entrepreneurs because they convince themselves that success isn't possible.

Optimist or Pessimist?

Would the people who know you best describe you as an optimistic or pessimistic person? Explain your response. _____

_____

_____

Use the thermometer below to identify your success instinct. How confident are you that you have what it takes to succeed?

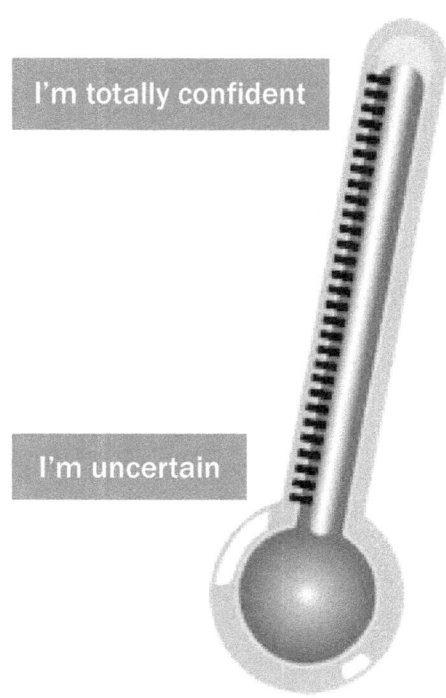

I'm totally confident

I'm uncertain

You Don't Need An Advanced Degree

What qualifications and/or expertise do you have that makes you the best candidate for starting a business? _____

_____

_____

_____

What do you believe is your income potential within the first year of operation? What is your potential within five years? Write your estimates below.

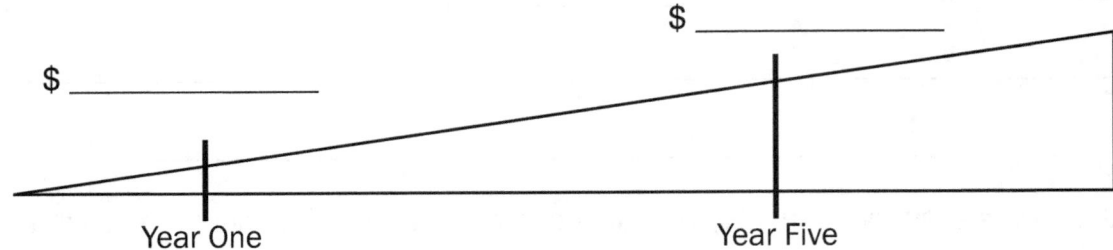

Continue to Improve

You might be an expert, but knowledge in today's world has a very short shelf life. If you aren't keeping up with developments and new ideas, you will quickly fall behind and become irrelevant.

What books or periodicals do you regularly read that will help you be a better leader and business person? _____

_____

_____

_____

Consider adding the following books to your reading list:

Good to Great   *How to Win Friends and Influence People*
21 Irrefutable Laws of Leadership   *Think and Grow Rich*
Entre-Leadership   *Built to Last*
The Lean Startup   *The Dip*
The Innovation Dilemma   *Start With Why*
The Leadership Challenge   *The Go-Giver*

In addition to books, you should consider subscribing to periodical such as *Success* magazine and *Entrepreneur* magazine.

What are a couple of personal weaknesses you need to address? _____

_____

What are you doing to address those weaknesses? _____

_____

_____

Find a Mentor or Coach

You can learn a lot from experienced entrepreneurs. You might be surprised at how willing they are to offer help, encouragement, and guidance. Consider people both inside and outside your field. Though you might not share common knowledge, there is great value in learning entrepreneurial principles from other entrepreneurs.

List three to five people who might be willing to mentor or coach you during the first two years of business. _____

_____

_____

_____

_____

Create Your Own Masters Degree

You don't have to enroll in a traditional university to get an education. Through sites such as Udemy and Coursera, you can have a custom-designed, world-class educational experience. A typical masters degree includes approximately 400 hours including classroom time and assignments. So, if you will invest one hour per day for two years in your entrepreneurial education, you can simulate a masters degree.

Core Curriculum

- **Leadership:** Identify and research books, courses, and seminars that will help you develop your leadership skills.

- **Communication:** Identify and research books, courses, and seminars that will help you develop your communication skills.

- **Organization and Time Management:** Identify and research books, courses, and seminars that will help you develop your organizational and time management skills.

- **Basic Accounting:** Identify and research books, courses, and seminars that will help you develop your accounting and financial skills.

- **Online Marketing:** Identify and research books, courses, and seminars that will help you develop your online marketing skills.

Evaluate your present level of knowledge in each area above using a scale from 1 to 10. Select educational tools that will help you move from your current knowledge level to mastery. You might find it necessary to select multiple tools to help you with areas where your knowledge level is weak.

Strong Work Ethic

I like what former Secretary of State, Colin Powell says about hard work as it relates to success, "A dream doesn't become reality through magic; it takes sweat, determination and hard work."

Describe your work ethic. Are you tenacious and focused? Do you fly by the seat of your pants? What do you expect to be your normal workday?_____

_____

_____

_____

Who do you expect to be the hardest working person in your business? _____

If the person listed above isn't you, your business is already at a disadvantage.

Each business requires a different time commitment needed to be successful. Some will require early mornings, and some, like restaurants, will require late evenings. The specifics are not important, other than that you have a commitment to work hard and take the lead at those crucial times.

If your business success is dependent upon your work ethic, how successful do you expect your business to be?

☐ I have a great work ethic so the business should be successful.

☐ I struggle with motivation, but I believe I can work hard and be successful.

☐ I'm hoping someone else will work hard to make my idea successful.

Are You A Problem Solver?

You probably already know this, but I'll repeat it anyway—problems are part of the entrepreneurial life. Come to think of it, problems are a part of everyone's life. Escaping problems isn't possible, therefore, we must learn to solve them.

Not all problems affect the bottom line, but every problem can affect the efficiency of your business. If you are a sole proprietor, the time you spend solving problems takes you away from the development of the business.

There are two characteristics common to successful entrepreneurs. Rate yourself in each category:

	never	sometimes	always
I learn from mistakes and don't repeat them.	|--------------------|	--------------------|	
I am willing to live with occasional failure.	|--------------------|	--------------------|	

Describe a recent problem-solving situation. Summarize your problem-solving approach.

_____

_____

_____

_____

_____

_____

_____

Review the process you used above and identify a three-step process that you can apply to almost any problem-solving situation.

1. _____

2. _____

3. _____

When you face a problem, are you energized or paralyzed? _____

How do you feel when you have solved a problem? _____

_____

_____

_____

_____

What are some topics or subjects about which you would like to become an expert?

1. _____

2. _____

3. _____

You can gain expertise through reading, attending a class, pursuing certification, or participating in online seminars. You don't have to create a business that no one is doing; you simply need to be ten percent better than everyone else.

Take some time to identify some books, classes, licenses, or certifications that would be beneficial to you and your business. List your ideas below: _____

_____

_____

_____

_____

PILLAR 2 ~ DEVELOP AN ACTIVE BUSINESS PLAN

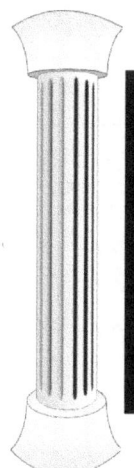
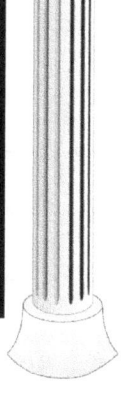

This lesson will help you assess the viability of your business idea. Plenty of good ideas for products and services never fly because there simply isn't a market for them—at least not a profitable one. You need to be as tough and honest about the viability of your business idea as you are about your basic qualifications to be the business owner. Avoid wishful thinking. "If you build it, they will come" isn't always true. They will come if the business foundation is sound and you build the business correctly.

Create A Business Plan

Every business—large or small—needs a business plan that provides a crystal clear picture of how your company will operate. Your business plan might encourage investors, inspire employees, and attract customers.

You've already worked on portions of the plan. We now need to assemble the business plan so that it makes sense to investors, bankers, and partners. Review the previous pages and create a document that answers (or leaves space for answers to) the following questions. Don't worry if you don't have answers to all of the questions yet. In upcoming lessons, we will deal with the missing information.

• What will your business do?

_____

_____

_____

What research confirms there is a demand for your business in the market?

_____

_____

_____

_____

- Who will be your competition and what are their strengths and weaknesses?

_____

_____

_____

_____

- What is your competitor's pricing structure?

_____

_____

_____

_____

- What will be your competitive advantage(s) and distinctions? (Why will customers choose you?)

_____

_____

_____

_____

- Who are your ideal customers and how are you going to market to them?

_____

_____

_____

_____

- What is your one year marketing plan?

_____

_____

_____

_____

- What skills or expertise do you need to hire?

_____

_____

_____

_____

- What will be all the costs to operate this business per week and month?

_____

_____

_____

_____

- Is your net income enough to pay you the income you wish to make?

_____

_____

_____

_____

- What are your mission, vision, and value statements?

_____

_____

_____

_____

_____

_____

_____

_____

_____

_____

- What are your one-year, three-year, and five-year goals for your company?

_____

_____

_____

_____

_____

_____

_____

_____

_____

_____

If you don't have time to create a business plan, you don't need to start a business!

Make An Exhaustive List Of Pre-Launch Tasks

Now that you have a business plan in place, let's move on to the process of starting up your business. Because your business is unique, your list of pre-launch tasks will be unique. Without exception, the next step was to formulate an exhaustive list of every possible thing that needed to be done prior to "turning the lights on" and serving the first paying customer.

Following are some universal tasks that apply to just about every business. Take a few moments to identify your plans for addressing these items. List your responses in the space provided.

Date you plan to have pre-launch tasks completed: _____

**already
complete**

☐   Business name:_____

☐   Tagline (service): _____

☐   Web domain: _____

- ☐ Website design: _____

- ☐ Corporation, partnership, sole proprietor? _____

- ☐ Licenses and permits: _____

- ☐ Business bank account: _____

- ☐ Physical location: _____

- ☐ Signage: _____

- ☐ Phone, office setup: _____

- ☐ Machinery, tools, equipment needed: _____

- ☐ Staffing needs: _____

- ☐ Other: _____

- ☐ Other: _____

- ☐ Other: _____

- ☐ Other: _____

- ☐ Other: _____

- ☐ Other: _____

List everything you can imagine needing to get your business operational. Return to the list frequently to make sure you are making progress. Don't attempt to start serving customers until all of the needs above (and any others you identify) are met.

Consider The Best Launch Season

There is a right and wrong time to start a business. Because business operates in predictable cycles, you need to plan your launch to capitalize on the strongest seasons. Starting your business at the wrong time can have long-lasting negative effects.

What is your primary product or service? _____

_____

When are people most likely to be looking for this product or service? _____

_____

_____

_____

What significant personal events do you anticipate over the next 36 months? _____

_____

_____

_____

Keep in mind, you want to be up and running when demand is at its peak. So, if you plan to start up a coffee shop, think about late summer. That way you'll have all the kinks worked out before getting into the busier fall season. Based on the information above, when is the best time to begin your business?

☐ Summer, specifically: _____

☐ Fall, specifically: _____

☐ Winter, specifically: _____

☐ Spring: specifically: _____

Conduct Basic Market Research

Just because you love golf and could use a driving range to improve your game, that doesn't mean a driving range is a good business idea. It shocks me how many businesses are started based purely on an individual's personal interests, and not good business sense.

Not every good idea is a good business idea. You can learn that by trial and error or you can conduct your own market research. Select one or more of the following to evaluate the viability of your business idea:

• Study research reports related to your product or service in your area.

• Conduct competitive intelligence by gathering information about the success of potential competitors in your market area.

- Choose people other than family and friends to take part in a test group to consider the need for your product or service.

- Develop variable approaches that can be adapted to produce the best profitability estimation.

Out of twenty random people, how many do you think need your product or service? ____

Why do they need it? _____

_____

Keep Your Business Model Simple

I think your first business should be simple, if at all possible. Sometimes we over complicate our business model. Start with a simple business model and add complexity in response to need, not desire. Many entrepreneurs make the mistake of creating the illusion of an organization when they are capable of handling the work alone or with limited help. Simple is better in every area. Your business model needs to encourage, not interfere with, success.

What is the simplest way you can provide your product or service? _____

_____

_____

What are the non-negotiable requirements for your business? _____

_____

_____

The simpler the operation, the lower your operating costs will be—and the higher your expected profits.

Fill A Need Or Meet A Desire

I have read many books on how to build and grow businesses. But when you get down to it, your business will either need to fill a need or meet a desire.

Need-based businesses deal with products like food, housing, and clothing. Or basic services like plumbing, electricity, or auto repair. Want-based businesses often deal with the same goods or services but at a higher level of satisfaction and luxury. People are motivated to buy a product, contract a service, or enroll in a class because of their real or perceived needs or desires. If your service doesn't fill a need or meet a desire, you will struggle to find customers.

Think about your business idea. What needs or desires does it address? _____

_____

_____

Rank the needs or desires listed on the previous page in order of priority in your business plan. What is your primary purpose?

1. _____

2. _____

3. _____

For each of the above, describe the profile of your target audience. _____

_____

_____

Is anyone else in your area offering a similar service or product? _____

If yes, what makes your product or service unique? _____

_____

Focus On Durable Goods And Services

Your product or service must be "durable." In other words, it should be in demand for a long time. Durability is another one of famed investor Warren Buffet's favorite qualities when investing in a

> You need a product/ service people want with a price they are willing to pay that allows you to make the net profit you need to meet your financial goals.

company. So as you would guess, he was not interested in investing in the Internet companies of the "dot com" era. He was criticized, but he had the last laugh. Do not get caught up in what is popular today.

Use the line below to evaluate the durability of your product or service. Place an X on the line indicating your opinion.

This is a fad <--> This is durable

What are two or three things you can do to make your product or service more durable?

_____

_____

_____

Why do you think your product or service will be needed ten years from now? _____

_____

_____

_____

There is always that rare company that initiates a new product or service, but it's an outlier. Don't over think business. In its simplest form you need a product/service people want with a price they are willing to pay that allows you to make the net profit you need to meet your financial goals. Master the fundamentals of start-up success. You can always venture out later with a solid track record and business foundation.

Unique Selling Proposition

Based on the answers you have just provided you now can form your USP (Unique Selling Proposition). The online Business Dictionary defines USP as real or perceived benefit of a good or service that differentiates it from the competing brands and gives its buyer a logical reason to prefer it over other brands.

> The Online Business Dictionary defines USP as real or perceived benefit of a good or service that differentiates it from the competing brands and gives its buyer a logical reason to prefer it over other brands.

What benefits is your company going to offer that your competition does not? _____

_____

_____

_____

_____

Model A Franchise

You can learn a lot about what is needed to operate a business like yours by reviewing the materials offered by franchisers. It's possible you won't initially need everything described in the brochures, but the information will help you identify some aspects of the business you might not have considered.

> You can learn a lot about what is needed to operate a business like yours by reviewing the materials offered by franchisers.

What are some franchises that offer a product or service similar to yours? _____

_____

_____

Identify some qualities of the franchise you'd like to incorporate into your business. _____

_____

_____

_____

_____

How do you plan to improve on what the franchise does? What will be your competitive advantage? _____

_____

_____

What are some other options you might consider? _____

_____

_____

_____

_____

Start A Business — Or Purchase One

There is a difference between a business owner and an entrepreneur. Entrepreneurs start businesses; owners own businesses. Purchasing an existing business has some of the same advantages as purchasing a franchise—established customer base, a history of earnings, etc. However, purchasing an existing business also carries with it any baggage associated with the previous owner.

List some businesses in your area that you would be interested in owning. _____

_____

_____

_____

What makes these businesses attractive to you? _____

_____

_____

List the pros and cons to purchasing an existing business. Pros: _____

_____

_____

Cons: _____

_____

_____

Buy The Company You Work For

This isn't always possible, but there are situations in which the owner is willing to sell the company to an employee. It is much like buying an existing company but with one huge advantage—your familiarity with the business and its customers. There are some things to consider. Rate yourself in each of the following areas with 1 being "not true" and 5 being "totally true."

	1	2	3	4	5
I love the company I work for	|	|	|	|	|
I have a good relationship with the owner	|	|	|	|	|
The business is healthy and profitable	|	|	|	|	|
The owner doesn't have a transition plan	|	|	|	|	|

Now, total your score: _____

If your score is 16-20, this is a real possibility.

If your score is 10-14, this is something to look into.

If your score is less than 10, you can look into it, but don't count on this working.

Review Your Idea Thoroughly

Don't be afraid to ask hard questions about your business idea. In doing so, you might discover some facts that will influence your decision. List some questions you should ask about every business idea. Use these questions to periodically evaluate every existing business and new idea.

1. _____

2. _____

3. _____

4. _____

5. _____

Don't Count On Venture Capital

Let me make this clear: You are not creating a business plan because you think you're going to get venture capital. Less than 1% of startup companies obtain money from venture capitalists. That means the competition for venture capital is fierce. The work you put into presenting your idea most likely won't land you an investment. Spend your time elsewhere.

Venture capital takes a substantial risk with the hope for a large gain. This group will often take an equity position in the company and may involve themselves in key company decisions. The fact is that some start-ups need substantial initial capital because they are bringing an invention into market. They may also be introducing a new industry, or an improvement in an existing industry.

Do you believe your idea is worthy of consideration by a venture capitalist? Why or why not? _____

_____

_____

_____

_____

Obtain Competitive Intelligence

Before starting a business, you must know everything you can about your competition. The more you know about your competition the better prepared your company will be to capitalize on their weaknesses.

Who are your top three competitors?

1. _____

2. _____

3. _____

As you think about your potential competitors, view their businesses through the following lens. Ask yourself these questions about every competitor.

1. How do they answer the phone and handle customer service?

2. How helpful is their website?

3. How accessible is the owner/operator?

4. Describe the quality of their products and/or services.

5. How do they price their products and services?

6. What are the strengths of the business?

7. What are the weaknesses of the business?

How will your business be different from their businesses? _____

_____

_____

_____

If you just plan to copy what someone else is doing, one of you is unnecessary.

Define Your Competitive Advantage

Every successful business has a competitive advantage over its competition. We see these advantages in a company's marketing strategy. Your competitive advantage must address a real or perceived need that your competition is ignoring. So, think about your potential competition. What needs among their customers are they ignoring? _____

_____

_____

At which of the following do you intend to be excellent?

☐ Price   ☐ Product or service options
☐ Speed of service   ☐ Customer service
☐ Quality   ☐ Other: _____

Why should a customer choose your company over another? If you don't know the answer to this question, then you should not be starting this company. Your competitive advantage can be broad in its scope, but these qualities are musts for success. I would also warn against customer service being your competitive advantage, as most companies think they are providing superior customer service compared to their competition. This is also an area that will take the longest, normally, to bear fruit.

Remember, your customers will ultimately decide if you are living up to your promises. Be careful not to promise things you can't incorporate into your business culture.

Mission Statement

One of the most important elements in your business plan is your mission statement. It describes the purpose of your company. It must be concise and memorable. It clearly describes your business and how you will provide value to your target customers.

Use the following questions to help craft your mission statement.

Who is your target customer or key market? _____

_____

What will you do or provide to your target customer or key market? _____

_____

What makes your product or service unique? _____

_____

What value will you provide to your target customer or key market? _____

_____

Now you have the necessary elements to create your mission statement. Use the space below to write your mission statement using the ideas expressed above._____

_____

_____

_____

Vision Statement

A mission statement focuses on what a company does and how it does it. A vision statement describes what you want the company to become. What do you see in three to five years? This is a verbal picture of your future expectations for your business. A mission statement is informational; a vision statement is inspirational.

If your company could achieve only one thing over the next five years, what would it be? _

_____

_____

You now have the foundation for your vision statement.

What is your vision for your business? _____

_____

_____

_____

Value Statement

Your value statement is the last piece of your company's declarations. The value statement is a set of core beliefs your company will operate by. These normally reflect the personal values of the owner or founder. You will have many opportunities to turn a profit, some of which will violate your core values.

A value statement describes the core beliefs by which your company operates. What are a few of your non-negotiable personal values? _____

_____

_____

How do you plan to incorporate these values into the culture of your company? _____

_____

_____

Rank the following values based on their importance to you with 1 being not important and 5 being critical.

	1	2	3	4	5
Integrity	|	|	|	|	|
Social responsibility	|	|	|	|	|
Profitability	|	|	|	|	|
Excellence	|	|	|	|	|
_____	|	|	|	|	|
_____	|	|	|	|	|
_____	|	|	|	|	|
_____	|	|	|	|	|

What is your value statement for your business? _____

_____

_____

_____

_____

PILLAR 3 ~ PROTECT YOURSELF AND YOUR BUSINESS

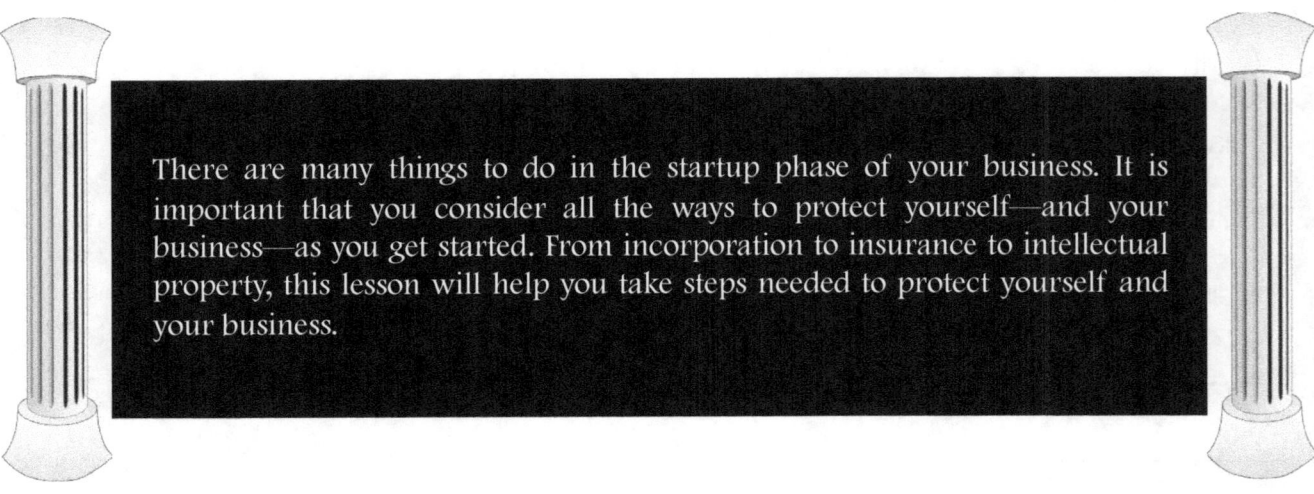

There are many things to do in the startup phase of your business. It is important that you consider all the ways to protect yourself—and your business—as you get started. From incorporation to insurance to intellectual property, this lesson will help you take steps needed to protect yourself and your business.

The owner of a corporation doesn't carry as much liability as a Sole Proprietor, both legally and financially. When you incorporate, you separate your personal belongings (home, cars, etc.) from your business. Therefore, if the business is sued or fails, your personal life is unaffected.

There are some additional benefits to being incorporated:
• Tax advantages
• Writing off health insurance premiums
• Savings on self-employment taxes
• Savings on life insurance

There are three basic types of corporations. Which best suits your business?

☐ C Corp is for larger companies that sell stock in their company and have over 100 shareholders.

☐ S Corp businesses can sell stock but have no more than 100 shareholders. The profits and losses are passed on to the business owner's personal income.

☐ LLC, which has always been the preferred choice for small businesses, does not have stock but pass all profits and losses to personal income.

What is your state's process for incorporating your business? _____

_____

_____

Purchase Insurance

It is a mistake to think you save money by having the bare minimum or no insurance at all. Insurance keeps you in business—as it only takes one catastrophe to bankrupt the business.

> **Insurance keeps you in business—as it only takes one catastrophe to bankrupt the business.**

Depending upon your business, there might be industry associations that offer discounts on insurance. You should be aware of the standard policies needed such as worker's compensation and general liability, but you should also consider getting a personal and business umbrella policy. It gives a final layer of protection.

Based on your business, what kinds of insurance do you need? _____

_____

_____

Who is your insurance agent and when are you scheduled to discuss your needs? _____

_____

> **To protect yourself and your family, you can purchase a health insurance plan with a very high deductible so that at least you have some protection.**

To protect yourself and your family, you can purchase a health insurance plan with a very high deductible so that at least you have some protection.

A high deductible plan allows you to have insurance in the event that something happens, but it will not cost much per month. When you talk to companies about health insurance, discuss the advantages of a Health Savings Account (HSA) plan. Also be sure to ask about preexisting condition limitations and specific aspects of the health plan.

Describe your personal health insurance situation. _____

_____

_____

_____

Insurance Checklist

Business owners can't afford to take risks that insurance can eliminate. Therefore, you need to have some specific insurance policies in place.

☐ General Liability Insurance: coverage that can protect you from a variety of claims including bodily injury, property damage, personal injury and others that can arise from your business operations.

☐ Workers Compensation Insurance: a form of insurance providing wage replacement and medical benefits to employees injured in the course of employment in exchange for mandatory relinquishment of the employee's right to sue his or her employer for the tort of negligence.

☐ Property Insurance: provides protection against most risks to property, such as fire, theft and some weather damage. This includes specialized forms of insurance such as fire insurance, flood insurance, earthquake insurance, home insurance, or boiler insurance.

☐ Commercial Auto Insurance: provides coverages such as liability, collision, comprehensive, medical payments (or personal injury protection) and uninsured motorist coverage for vehicles used in a business.

☐ Liability Umbrella Insurance: This is extra liability insurance. It is designed to help protect you from major claims and lawsuits and, as a result, it helps protect your assets and your future.

Protect Your Name

Can you and did you obtain a domain for the exact way you spell and use your company name? _____

_____

Have you service marked your name with your state corporation commission? _____

_____

_____

_____

_____

Protect Your Intellectual Property

Intellectual property refers to a name, logo, trade secret, published work, or invention. It is the result of your creativity; therefore, it has value and must be protected. Other common types of intellectual property include copyrights, patents, industrial design rights, and trade secrets, which apply in some jurisdictions.

Trademarking, trade secrets, and patents seem to be the ones that apply most in businesses. There are subtle but important differences between these types of protection that you need to learn and apply to your specific business situation.

What intellectual property do you need to protect? _____

_____

_____

_____

_____

_____

Do you have any inventions, unique processes, or competitive advantages that warrant being protected? _____ Yes _____ No

If You Partner, Consider These Rules

If you have chosen a partnership, there are some rules to follow. Sadly, I have learned all these rules the expensive way. Going into a business partnership is very similar to a marriage. In the beginning, you will spend more time talking to and being around this person than your spouse. Before starting a partnership, do the following:

• Negotiate what the buyout would be well before you start the business.

• Write out the terms of your partnership agreement and have it reviewed by an attorney.

• Develop an appropriate non-compete and/or nondisclosure agreement. This protect the business from competition started by one of the partners.

If you are considering a partnership, what makes your partner a good fit? _____

_____

_____

_____

Who will be responsible for what? List responsibilities for each partner. _____

_____

_____

_____

_____

It is best to write out the basic terms of your partnership agreement and have it reviewed by an attorney. If you cannot afford an attorney, at the very least, get this agreement notarized.

Establish The Proper Legal Framework

You need to be aware of all needed licenses, permits, and certifications for the industry you are entering. You can usually find these out by going to your local business tax office or contacting your local Chamber of Commerce.

If at all possible, obtain all the licenses yourself as soon as you can. Don't wait. Failure to obtain all of the proper licenses can prevent your form opening your doors on your anticipated target date. Remember: government bureaucracies can be painfully slow. Allow for additional time beyond the timeframes stated when obtaining the licenses you need.

Which of the following do you need?

☐ Local licenses, permits and registrations

☐ Employer Identification Number, or EIN

☐ Professional licenses

☐ State tax license

> **Failure to obtain all of the proper licenses can prevent your form opening your doors on your anticipated target date.**

☐ State labor department registration (required by most, but not all, states)

☐ Liquor license (only as applicable)

☐ Other: _____

How long will it take to get your legal framework in place? _____

_____

Know All Applicable Labor Laws

As a business owner, you must adhere to all labor laws. Unfortunately, these can be confusing and complex. However, violating these laws can have catastrophic consequences. Here are four specific categories of labor laws that you should note:

• Hiring discrimination. Under federal law, you cannot hire employees based only on their gender, race, ethnicity, marital status, or sexual orientation.

• Child labor. Under the Fair Labor Standards Act, it is unlawful to employ children younger than 14 in nonagricultural occupations. Children 14-15 can be employed outside school hours for limited periods of time. 16 and 17-year-olds can be hired in any occupation other than those deemed "hazardous."

• Independent contractors. The IRS has established guidelines to determine whether an employee is a regular employee (part-time or full-time) or a contract worker.

• Immigration law. Businesses must keep an up-to-date "I-9" form—which verifies a worker's legal citizenship or immigration status—on file for every employee.

Review the labor laws above. Which do you believe will affect your business? _____

_____

_____

Check with the Small Business Administration office near you for information and advice regarding labor laws.

PILLAR 4 ~ RECRUIT A TEAM YOU CAN TRUST

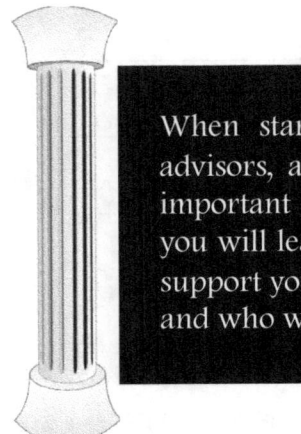

When starting a business, your team consists of staff, professional advisors, and mentors. Building a successful team is one of the most important things that will lead to your business' success. In this lesson you will learn how to find, and surround yourself with people who will support your idea, respect your leadership, who you will work well with, and who will provide helpful guidance.

Qualify Your Labor Market

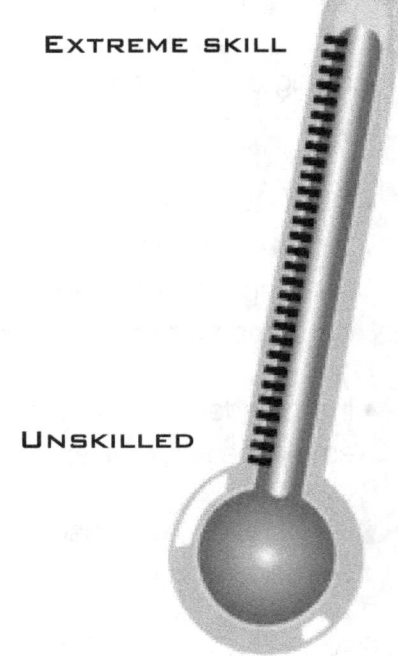

EXTREME SKILL

Think about your business and determine the level of skill needed to keep it functioning efficiently. Using the thermometer to the right, indicate how skilled you need your employees to be.

List the specific skills you need to have on your team. For instance, do you need a web developer, electrician, or human resources director? _____

_____

_____

_____

UNSKILLED

What are five questions you will ask every potential employee?

1. _____

2. _____

3. _____

4. _____

5. _____

How will you find skilled employees? _____

_____

_____

Why will potential employees want to be a part of your company? _____

_____

_____

Try To Hire The Best, Regardless

Make it your mission to surround yourself with the most talented, smartest, experienced and competent team of employees you can find—and make sure you actually look for them. Sadly, it is all too common for new business owners to hire family members and friends, either out of a sense of obligation or by default.

> Make it your mission to surround yourself with the most talented, smartest, experienced and competent team of employees you can find.

What characteristics are you looking for in potential employees? _____

_____

_____

How will you determine if people embody those characteristics? _____

_____

_____

Try to hire staff that is outside your immediate comfort zone. The main criterion is whether they will add value you your company. Do not be intimidated or threatened because someone is older with twenty years more experience than you.

Let more experienced employees know that you value their input, but expect their full support for the decisions that you alone are authorized to make. Remember—and don't be afraid to gently remind them—you're the boss.

There Are Mechanics To Hiring

Draw a flowchart below that describes your hiring process.

Which of the following do you already have in place?

☐ A list of questions to ask prospective employees (see the next section).

☐ A job description for every position in the company.

☐ An employment letter outlining the 30-day probationary period, expectations, benefits, etc.

☐ A list of questions to ask references.

☐ A form letter to send those you chose not to hire.

☐ A clear understanding of the questions NOT to ask during the interview process.

☐ A clearly-defined process to follow in the event you need to dismiss an employee.

Start now creating the information listed above that you do not yet have in place. Then, put together an employment folder or manual so that your hiring process is simple and consistent.

Approach Staffing Strategically

Create an organizational chart that identifies the full-time and part-time positions you need in your business. Draw the chart in the space below.

Every employee is a walking-and-talking company representative. Those with direct and sustained contact with your customers should strongly reflect your company's business ethos.

How important is it for you to like the people on your team? Mark your response on the line below.

Not important   Very important

$$\longleftarrow\hspace{10cm}\longrightarrow$$

Are there other people you need to involve in the hiring process? If so, who are they? ____

_____

_____

If You Don't Have The Skills, Partner

You might think that having a strong background in the industry that you're planning to enter is essential. Not necessarily.

If you can find a partner with the background you lack, you may be more prepared than you realize. Expertise in your industry is a pre-requisite for starting a successful business. If you don't have it, make sure to partner with, or hire, someone who does.

> Expertise in your industry is a pre-requisite for starting a successful business.

What are your personal strengths and how do they position your company for success? __

_____

_____

_____

What are your personal weaknesses? In what areas of business are you most unsure? __

_____

_____

_____

Who are some people you might want to bring alongside to work in your areas of weakness? _____

_____

_____

_____

> In the end, a partnership is a mutual learning experience.

You need to learn the business in your own right, and your partner, however experienced, won't have all the answers. Make sure your partnership agreement clarifies how business decisions are to be made. In the end, a partnership is a mutual learning experience.

Lead Like A Coach

When your business starts, it will function a lot like preseason workouts for a football team. You'll quickly identify the areas that need work and you will need to address those areas with encouragement and motivation. You need to coach your employees.

What are some characteristics of great coaches? _____

_____

_____

List the characteristics on the lines below and rate yourself in each area with 1 being poor and 5 being excellent.

	1	2	3	4	5
Listening skills					
Motivation					
Powerful questioning skills					
Creative thinking					
Strong leadership					
Flexibility					
Problem solving					
Delegating					
Recruiting					
Calmness under pressure					
Communication					
Teaching					

Which characteristics need the most work? _____

_____

_____

What is your plan for addressing those areas? _____

_____

_____

Maximize The Talent Of Your Employees

To be a great leader you must be able to place people where they will be most productive. Successful business owners will maximize the talent of their employees. It is your job to know what each person's talent is and to place him or her in a position to thrive.

Consider the organizational chart you developed in a previous step. What are three things you can do to bring out the best in your employees?

1. _____

2. _____

3. _____

What are some things you can do to maintain employee morale and devotion? _____

_____

_____

_____

_____

_____

_____

Build And Trust Your "Cabinet"

The cabinet is the president's "go-to" team. All decisions will go through one or more of these individuals. Your initial support team usually consist of an accountant, lawyer, banker, and bookkeeper. Over time, this group might include key leaders from your staff.

How confident are you that your "cabinet" agrees with your Value Statement?

Not confident   Very confident

$$\longleftrightarrow$$

What specialists do you need to hire or contract? _____

_____

_____

_____

_____

Get To Know Your Local Bank

It's tempting to shop around for the cheapest banking options, but that's not always the wisest thing to do. If you cultivate a relationship with a local bank, you will find that relationship paying huge dividends down the road. You'll still have to apply for loans and adhere to government regulations regarding financial matters, but your banker can help you navigate the otherwise confusing waters of paperwork and bureaucracy.

Which bank do you think is the best choice for your business services? _____

_____

_____

_____

_____

Develop A Support Group

It's important to have one or more people in your life that can help you achieve your business dreams. We all need mentors and cheerleaders.

Who are three people you can include in your support group? _____

_____

_____

_____

_____

The following organizations also might be helpful in providing support. Which of these are available in your area?

☐ SCORE

☐ A business owners group

☐ Business coaches

☐ Other business leaders

PILLAR 5 ~ BUILD A BRAND

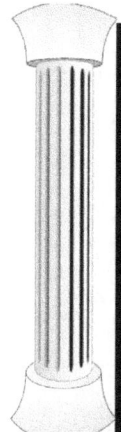
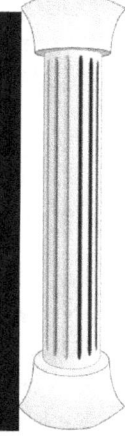

If you don't find customers for your product or service, you unfortunately will not stay in business for long. Marketing is all about knowing who your ideal customer is, deciding what means of advertising will best reach this group with the message you have determined will make them use your product or service. This lesson will help you create your marketing plan, and think through specifics of your business name, website, taglines, and more. After completing the Action Steps in this section, you will walk away with a better plan for reaching the right customers and keep them coming back for more.

Start Branding From Day One

Branding is a promise you make to your customers about an important quality or attribute they can expect to receive from using your product or service.

People often remember your branding better than they remember your products or services. They know if you have delivered on the promises you made and their future business is dependent upon that information. So, you can't go into the branding process haphazardly. You must be intentional about establishing your business identity in such a way that you can deliver on the promises you make.

> Branding is a promise you make to your customers.

What promise are you making in conjunction with your product or service? _____

_____

_____

_____

_____

Which of the following characteristics should be included in your branding?

☐ Durability

☐ Low prices

☐ Locally made or grown

☐ Handcrafted

☐ Fast

☐ Convenient

☐ Professional

☐ Other: _____

Which of the characteristics above need to be included in your branding? Circle two or three.

Now, using the words circled above, create a short, concise statement that describes your competitive advantage. _____

_____

_____

What Do You Remember?

There are plenty of examples of great branding. We often use familiar brand names to describe categories… we Xerox a document or apply a Band-Aid to a cut. You probably remember several tag lines or jingles associated with products you use or advertisements you frequently see or hear.

Do you remember these companies and their tag lines?

- Lexus - Pursuit of Perfection

- Nike - Just Do It

- Papa John's - Better Pizza, Better Ingredients, Papa John's

- Apple - Think Different

- McDonalds - I'm Lovin' It

- Lay's Chips - Betcha Can't Eat Just One

- State Farm Insurance - Like a Good Neighbor, State Farm Is There

Think of some companies you know for their branding or tag lines. List a few examples in the space below. _____

_____

_____

_____

_____

What one quality—if your company could deliver—would set you apart from your competition? _____

_____

What is the number one benefit of using your product or service? _____

_____

_____

_____

Your responses to these questions are the beginning of your branding process.

What's In A Name? A Lot.

The naming of your business is more important than you might think. A non-Internet business should have a name that clearly tells the customer what kind of business it is, and the type of service it provides. If your business is Internet-based, aim for something memorable and unique.

Think about some businesses in your area. What are some names that communicate with clarity? What is it about those company names that makes you want to visit them? _____

_____

_____

_____

Are you planning for your company to expand into other areas or will it remain in one location? _____ expand _____ remain in one location

If you already have a name, write it here: _____

List three possible names and ask close friends and acquaintances to help you evaluate the possibilities. Keep in mind the fact that changing the name of your company after it is established can be an expensive process.

1. _____

2. _____

3. _____

Now, go back to the list and rank the potential name ideas in order from first to last. Eliminate the third choice and do more evaluations of the remaining two options. Within a couple of days, you should have a winning name for your business.

Potential name is _____

Final Name Qualifiers

☐ Have you checked with your State Corporation Commission to see if it is available?

☐ Are there any businesses with similar names in your area or industry?

☐ Before finalizing a name is the domain name available (.com)?

☐ If you answered yes to the above questions you have your name

☐ Purchase your domain name (check and make sure you have spelled it correctly before final purchase).

☐ Now you are ready to incorporate your business.

Elevator Pitch

This is a drill down on your USP (Unique Sales Proposition) from earlier in the workbook. What is it that your company offers (product or service) and why should customer's choose you over your competition? You need to be able to own some simple statements that communicate this in a way that makes prospective customer's want to know more about your company.

What problems do you think you can solve better or faster then your competition? _____

_____

_____

Write an elevator pitch you and your employees will commit to memory. _____

_____

_____

_____

_____

Develop A Tag Line

A tagline is a short, catchy phrase that emphasizes a quality of service or a promise your company will deliver. Think about some of the catchy tag lines you know. List a few below.

_____

_____

Now identify a couple of promises your company will deliver or a quality of service you intend to provide. List them here. _____

_____

_____

Use the space below to list some tagline possibilities. Review these with your closest advisors and select the one that is most appropriate. _____

_____

_____

_____

What Makes a Great Tag Line or Slogan?

A tag line or clever slogan can be one of the most powerful marketing tools you have. Unfortunately, many people don't give much thought to their development. As we've already seen, a powerful tag line or slogan can establish your competitive advantage. You aren't developing a catchy phrase; you are telling the world what makes your company unique. Here are some characteristics of a great tag line or slogan:

☐ It differentiates you from your competition.

☐ It brags a little.

☐ It sets a high standard.

☐ It is memorable.

☐ It includes a key benefit.

☐ It creates a positive feeling.

As you think about your business, what do you want your tag line or slogan to communicate: _____

_____

_____

Marketing Is More Than A Business Card

Many businesses fail because they under-budget for marketing. I am a big fan of word-of-mouth, but it is rare that this can bring in enough customers to build a successful company.

Which of the following are elements of your marketing strategy?

☐ Website

☐ Business cards

☐ Newspaper advertisements

☐ Radio or television ads

☐ Social media (Facebook, Twitter, Pinterest)

☐ Online marketing

☐ Direct Mail

☐ Others: _____

What are some creative ways you can market your business? _____

_____

_____

_____

_____

What percentage of your net profit do you plan to invest in marketing? _____

Nimble small business owners help sponsor and show up for important local events, including music festivals and fairs. They register with the Chamber of Commerce and go out of their way to become known in their community. Be pro-active and visible, not just hoping people will spread the word for you.

Build A Great Website

Many would-be small business owners wonder whether they need an online presence. If they are doing all of their business locally, they figure that traditional advertising should be enough. Moreover, if none of their products or services will ever be sold online, they see even less reason to invest in a web site.

> A web site is an integral part of business marketing and advertising.

A web site is an integral part of business marketing and advertising. Most of your prospective customers—even those born during the heyday of radio and television—are surfing the Internet. Developing an online presence is as essential as having a business card. Prospective customers should be able to find your products and services described there, as well as basic contact information.

Use the following checklist to develop a basic web presence. You can add additional pages and information as needed.

- ☐ Homepage design
- ☐ Products and services
- ☐ Contact information

- ☐ Information about the company and/or owner
- ☐ Mission and value statements
- ☐ Photos of location, staff, and products

How would you describe the websites of your competitors? _____

_____

_____

_____

How can you meet your customers' needs and expectations through your website? _____

_____

_____

_____

Do you have the ability to build a basic website or do you need to hire someone to do it for you? If you need to hire someone, ask family members and friends. You might find a high school student or college student who is willing to take on the project for a little spending money. Regardless of who you choose, create an agreement that establishes the timeline for completion and payment. Consider a down payment of 50% with the balance paid upon completion.

> You might find a high school student or college student who is willing to take on the project for a little spending money.

Join Business Associations

A simple way to build credibility and to learn more about your industry is to join associations. These are also a great way to learn what is working for others within your industry. They may also offer discounts on products and professional services you may need.

> General associations like the Chamber of Commerce may be good for networking and sharing local marketing tips.

General associations like the Chamber of Commerce may be good for networking and sharing local marketing tips. However, Industry-specific associations might help with labor recruitment, training, getting involved in lobbying and keeping up on changes to regulations and other important industry news.

List some associations available in your area:

1. _____

2. _____

3. _____

What are some national associations dedicated to your area of expertise?

1. _____

2. _____

3. _____

Talk to other business owners in your area and industry. Find out what associations they are actively involved in. Ask which associations they find worthwhile and why.

What benefits might you gain from joining one or more associations? _____

_____

_____

_____

_____

_____

_____

Systematically Survey Customers

Customer feedback is crucial to being a successful company. There are several ways you can distribute surveys. If you keep the survey short, you can use a card at the point of sale or provide a postage paid card to be returned in the mail.

Use email lists to send out surveys created with online tools such as wufoo.com or surveymonkey.com. When you analyze the data, report the summary on your website and in other advertising pieces.

Before you send out a survey, you need to identify the information you want to gather from customers. The survey must be no longer than five questions and able to be completed in five minutes or less. You might consider offering incentives for completion of the survey. Offer a discount coupon or free item when surveys are submitted.

> Before you send out a survey, you need to identify the information you want to gather from customers. The survey must be no longer than five questions and able to be completed in five minutes or less.

Below are some possible questions to ask on the survey. Mark the five questions that best suit your business.

☐ Did the product/service meet your expectations?

☐ Would you use our company or buy our product again?

☐ Would you refer our product or service to a friend? Why or why not?

☐ Do you have a specific concern that needs to be addressed?

☐ How helpful was our staff?

☐ How friendly was the staff?

☐ Were you welcomed upon arrival at our business location?

☐ How long did you wait before being served?

☐ What additional products or services do you want us to provide?

☐ How likely are you to do business with us again?

Develop Customer Testimonies

Customer testimonies are a powerful tool for businesses. Potential customers like seeing and hearing from people who have done business with you. Testimonies are easy to obtain because of the proliferation of phones that shoot video and record audio.

Below are some additional sources of testimonies. Which ones do you already have in place?

- ☐ Facebook Reviews.
- ☐ LinkedIn Reviews.
- ☐ YouTube Video Reviews.
- ☐ Local Search Directories.
- ☐ Other: _____

Why would customer reviews help build your business? _____

_____

_____

_____

_____

_____

List ten people you can ask for testimonies before starting your business. Consider this your pilot group.

1. _____   6. _____

2. _____   7. _____

3. _____   8. _____

4. _____   9. _____

5. _____   10. _____

Look For Added Value

Can your product perform more functions than the competition? Do you offer additional complimentary services? Consider how you might bring additional value to your customers. A fresh competitive advantage might also allow you to increase your prices.

Use the pyramid diagram below to identify the added value you can provide through your business. Begin at the bottom with the basic product or service. Then, work your way to the top adding value by adding additional services.

_____

_____

_____

_____

_____

Added value

Added value

Added value

Added value

Basic product or service

Which of the added value items on the previous page do you believe you can deliver? ____

_____

_____

_____

_____

_____

Try to think broadly in terms of its branding or competitive advantage potential. If customers consistently say, "Oh yeah, that's the company that offers that special extra," you are on your way to something exciting. Once you have determined how you will add value, communicate it in your marketing.

Promote "Word Of Mouth"

Create a product or service that people want to tell others about. It will become advertising that you won't have to pay for. In today's world of *Twitter* and *Facebook*, your customers will remark about your business. You get to decide if those remarks will be positive or negative. You can't neglect the power of the Internet—positive and negative.

> I am a big fan of word-of-mouth, but it is rare that this can bring in enough customers to build a successful company.

You can enhance your market share by having positive comments about your business in social media. Likewise, your brand can suffer harm if there is negativity on social media. Encourage your customers to leave reviews on Google, Yelp, and other sites where other people might look for information about your business.

List some people you can enlist as "ambassadors" for your business. Select people who have an audience and are well-respected among your target customers.

1. _____

2. _____

3. _____

What do you want people to say about your product or service? _____

_____

_____

_____

_____

What are three things you can do to make sure these comments are accurate?

1. _____

2. _____

3. _____

You can also try to cultivate some key "influentials" early on. These are people who, by virtue of their position in a community, naturally tend to speak to lots of other people and whose opinions may be highly valued. If they are familiar with your pricing and product, and are sold on your company, they can spread the word "virally"—perhaps through a blog, Facebook, or another community-based information network. This is why you have to be a people person.

Develop A Startup Story

People, especially Americans, love stories of humble beginnings and creative vision. You may or may not fit this mold, but I bet you have a story to tell. Here are some ways to tell your story. Select the ones that are applicable to your situation.

> If people are familiar with your pricing and product, and are sold on your company, they will spread the word virally.

☐ Craft a professional press release.

☐ Become a guest on a local radio show.

☐ Identify with charitable causes in your area. People like to believe they are spending their money with someone who cares for their community.

☐ Place your startup story on your website as a video interview.

☐ Write an article to submit to your local paper. Explain how many jobs you hope to create and the impact you hope to have on the community.

☐ Other ideas: _____

What about your company or yourself is interesting and would make a good story? _____

_____

_____

_____

_____

_____

Leverage Social Media

Businesses can use social media to build community around their products and services. Because community is vital in today's marketing strategy, using social media is no longer an option; it is required for people who want to reach potential customers in the way those people receive information.

Your brand—whether it is a business or your personality—needs to have a presence in the social media world. New technologies are being developed that entrepreneurs are using with great success. The standard social media services are Twitter, Facebook, Pinterest, etc. There are "new" players in the market, too. Check out Instagram and Periscope to see if they might offer you some benefit.

List below the social media services you believe can benefit your business. _____

_____

_____

_____

What would you hope to accomplish through using social media to reach your customers?

_____

_____

_____

Develop An Image

Your goal, with your logo and color scheme, is to create a professional image. If you hope to own a successful business, it needs to look like one from day one. To keep it simple, respond to the following:

• What color or colors do you want in the logo? _____

• What look are you hoping to portray? Will it be modern, classic, retro, etc.? _____

_____

Sketch a few logo ideas below. Don't worry about your art ability. Just express your ideas.

Mark through the ideas that won't translate well to printed materials, T-shirts, and uniforms.

Rate your logo idea based on the following criteria with 1 being poor and 5 being excellent.

	1	2	3	4	5
Simplicity	|	|	|	|	|
Adaptability	|	|	|	|	|
Timelessness	|	|	|	|	|
Adaptability	|	|	|	|	|
Uniqueness	|	|	|	|	|
Adaptability	|	|	|	|	|
Appropriateness	|	|	|	|	|

Review this lesson and fine tune your ideas. This is a critical part in the building of your business. This is one area where it might be helpful to hire a pro. You can't neglect this part of the process.

PILLAR 6 ~ DEVELOP SYSTEMS

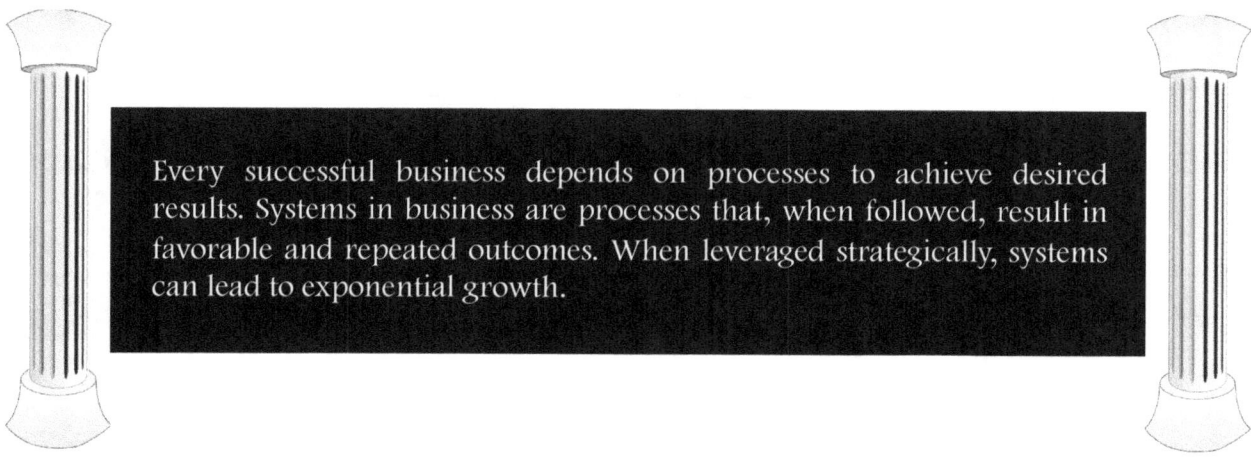

Every successful business depends on processes to achieve desired results. Systems in business are processes that, when followed, result in favorable and repeated outcomes. When leveraged strategically, systems can lead to exponential growth.

Identify Your Recipes

Business success isn't a coincidence; it takes intentionality and focus. Repeated business success means keeping track of what you've been doing so you can replicate it or replace it in the future.

> Business success isn't a coincidence; it takes intentionality and focus.

Too many entrepreneurs have the same answer to the question, "How did you reach this level of success?" Their response is telling—"I don't know, it just happened." No it didn't. There were things they tried that worked. Some efforts failed. Others needed tweaking. Entrepreneurs must know what worked and what didn't work.

I'm convinced this is the reason many new businesses fail. It's easy to associate success with the wrong variable and, as a result, repeat an action that negatively affects the bottom line.

For instance, if a business owner signs up for an advertising package with the local newspaper and starts an email list at the same time, he or she must be able to discern which one is producing the most beneficial results. This is a system that must be tracked.

There are other systems or processes that require constant attention. Though you might not know the answers to these questions now, you will need to monitor your business so you have an accurate and current understanding of what is happening.

◆ What is the primary source of your customers/clients?

◆ Which days and times produce the heaviest walk-in or online traffic?

◆ How does blogging and social media affect business activity?

◆ What percentage of your gross receipts is being invested in advertising and marketing?

◆ How do printed or online coupons affect business?

◆ What are customers/clients saying about your products or services?

List below some statistics you plan to track. _____

_____

_____

_____

_____

What do you plan to learn from the statistics identified above? _____

_____

_____

_____

Prepare to Train

When a business starts out, processes aren't very obvious. However, the more your business grows, the more you will need processes and the best time to create them is before you need them.

Training is a key ingredient in the business process. You might need to train contract workers or employees how to do their jobs. You might need to train customers how to interact with your business. At some point, you will become a trainer, so you need to prepare for it now.

Think about your business three years from now and list below some of the tasks that will be part of an average day. _____

_____

_____

_____

_____

Using the list you just created, identify the training topics you will need to cover. _____

_____

_____

_____

_____

_____

_____

_____

Training can be delivered in a variety of ways. You can train personally, hire a trainer, or deliver training online. This is one area where it pays to get the help of a professional. Bad training is no more effective than not training at all.

Who are some people you can turn to for help developing your training program? _____

_____

_____

_____

_____

Don't Become Dependent

Do not allow yourself to be too dependent on others. You must maintain control of your business and be aware of what is happening. Don't let your business be hampered by the departure of an employee. As the owner, you must be willing and able to step in and fill the gap when needed.

> You must maintain control of your business and be aware of what is happening.

What information about your company do you need to receive daily? _____

_____

_____

_____

What information do you need monthly? _____

_____

_____

_____

What combinations, pass codes, passwords, etc. do you need to have full access to all vital information? _____

_____

_____

_____

_____

Dealing With Complaints

Very few things can be more draining to a business owner than dealing with an upset customer. Your staff needs to know you are available to back them up or to step into a tense situation.

Complaint Solving Process

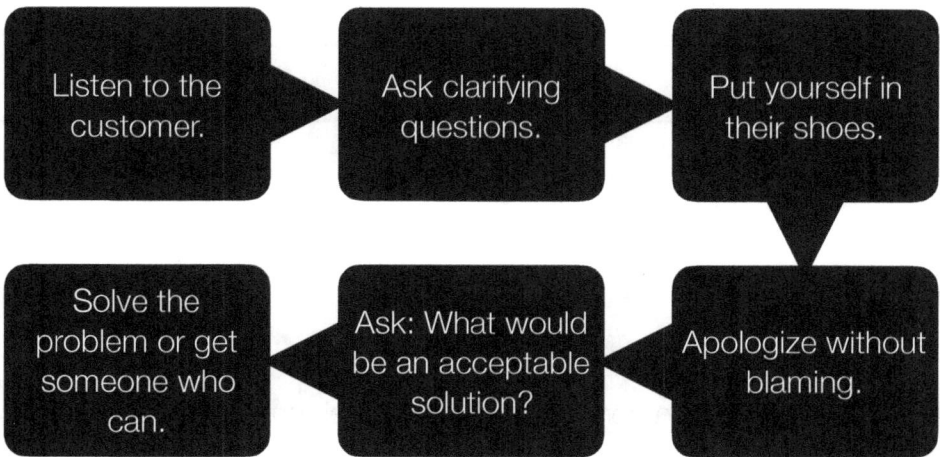

Believe it or not, listening to an intelligent unsatisfied customer might help you to better run your business. Another benefit of dealing with complaints is that you can see weaknesses in your process or products that can be rectified.

What can you learn from dissatisfied customers? _____

_____

_____

_____

_____

Describe a time when a complaint of yours was well-handled. _____

_____

_____

_____

_____

_____

What did you learn from that experience? _____

_____

_____

_____

_____

Everything discussed in this lesson contributes to the development of the systems and processes that will undergird your business in the years ahead. Don't overlook the significance of this step in the entrepreneurial journey.

PILLAR 7 ~ KNOW YOUR NUMBERS

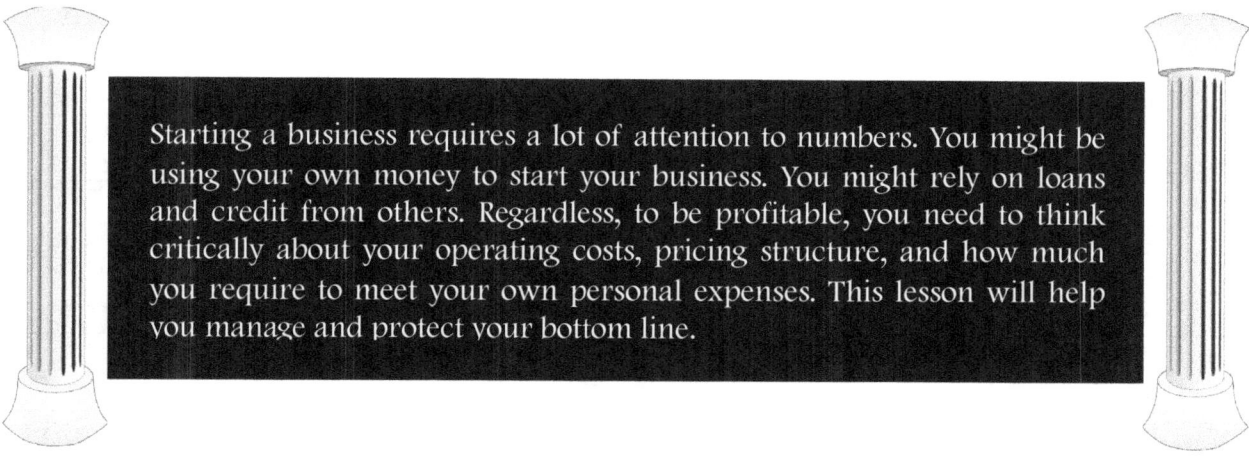

Starting a business requires a lot of attention to numbers. You might be using your own money to start your business. You might rely on loans and credit from others. Regardless, to be profitable, you need to think critically about your operating costs, pricing structure, and how much you require to meet your own personal expenses. This lesson will help you manage and protect your bottom line.

Reserves

One of the best ways to build your business is to try to insulate it against the threat of destruction. In other words, you need to have enough cash on hand to cover any potential shortfalls in revenue. The reserve is there in the event of an emergency. It can be large or small at the outset, but it should be equal to your operating expenses for a projected period of interruption in which your business may be unable to generate new income.

Based on your monthly operating budget, what is a healthy three-month reserve?

_____

Based on the amount of money you have on hand, how long could your business survive with no revenue?

☐ Six months or longer
☐ Three to six months
☐ One to three months
☐ Less than a month

What is your emergency plan in the event everything that possibly could go wrong goes wrong? _____

_____

_____

Credit Is Your Lifeblood

Credit is the lifeblood of your business, as it keeps all the vital organs of your business functioning. If you are giving customers 30 days to pay their invoices, you will need credit to operate while waiting for these payments.

What is your personal attitude toward credit? _____

_____

_____

_____

How have you handled credit in your personal life?

☐ I don't use credit

☐ I've never had a problem

☐ I have had some issues in the past

☐ My personal credit is really messed up

You need to realize the connection between the way you handle personal credit and the way you will handle business credit. Irresponsibility in one leads to irresponsibility in the other.

What potential capital expenses are connected to your business? _____

_____

_____

_____

In the event you needed to make a large capital purchase, how would you pay for it? ____

_____

_____

_____

Take A Modest Salary

New business owners tend to pay themselves too much salary initially when their startup money is coming from someone else. Some experts suggest paying yourself whatever is left after all other expenses are paid.

What annual salary do you need from your business? _____

What adjustments can you make in your lifestyle so that you can reduce the amount of salary you need from the business? _____

_____

_____

The SBA offers some commonsensical advice on this issue: "If you are still in startup mode and have no profit history or aren't turning a profit yet, you might want to set your salary by reviewing your own personal costs. What do you need to support your modest, startup lifestyle? Defer everything above and beyond that."

Avoid Unnecessary Expenses

I am not a big fan of starting a company without having some of your own money at risk. I think it helps to have a little "skin in the game." As I suspect that you'll manage your own money better than money from an outside source.

Always think lean. Subject every prospective expense to the acid test. Is this outlay really needed to accomplish the goals I have for my company? Is it a vanity expense? Is this the best time to make this purchase? If I can't defer it, how can I do it more cheaply?

Take a close look at your startup expenses and identify those that are absolutely critical and those that are optional. Be honest about your need for the things on the list. Look for free or inexpensive ways to handle some expenses.

Which of your startup expenses are optional? _____

_____

_____

_____

What anticipated purchases can be delayed until your business becomes profitable? _____

_____

_____

Focus On Net Profit

Your net profit is the number you want to keep track of. This could be called your business "batting average." The easiest way to keep this number high is to keep your labor and fixed expenses low.

> The easiest way to keep your net profit high is to keep your labor and fixed expenses low.

You want to guard your net profit and keep this percentage as high as possible. Gross profit is what you bring in before expenses (Gross profit = sales – cost of goods sold). If you aren't making a net profit, your business is headed in the wrong direction.

What do you estimate to be your net profit during your first year? _____

What do you estimate to be your net profit during your second year? _____

Here is the basic way to find out your net profit:

• Step 1: What are the total sales for your business? _____

• Step 2: Add all other revenues received: _____

• Step 3: Subtract the amount of all of your business expenses _____

• Step 4: This is your net profit: _____

You can reverse the process above to establish sales goals based on the desired net profit.

Do you believe your business can meet your net profit expectations? _____

Explain your response. _____

_____

_____

Guard Your Accounts Receivable

Money people owe you isn't income until you actually receive payment. Before starting your business, you must establish guidelines for customer payments. Allow as little time as possible between delivery of goods or services and receipt of payment.

How long will you allow people to submit payment? _____

What is your plan for pursuing payment from customers who are late? _____

_____

_____

Use Dashboards

A business dashboard is an information management tool that is used to track key data relevant to business performance. Through the use of data visualizations, dashboards simplify complex data sets to provide users with at a glance awareness of current performance.

Dashboards, simply put, are visual snapshots that help entrepreneurs see how their business compares to projections or goals. A dashboard can represent any measurable data—income, customers, net profit, refunds, etc. If you do a web search for business dashboards, you will find plenty of examples to get you started.

PILLAR 8 ~ CHANGE

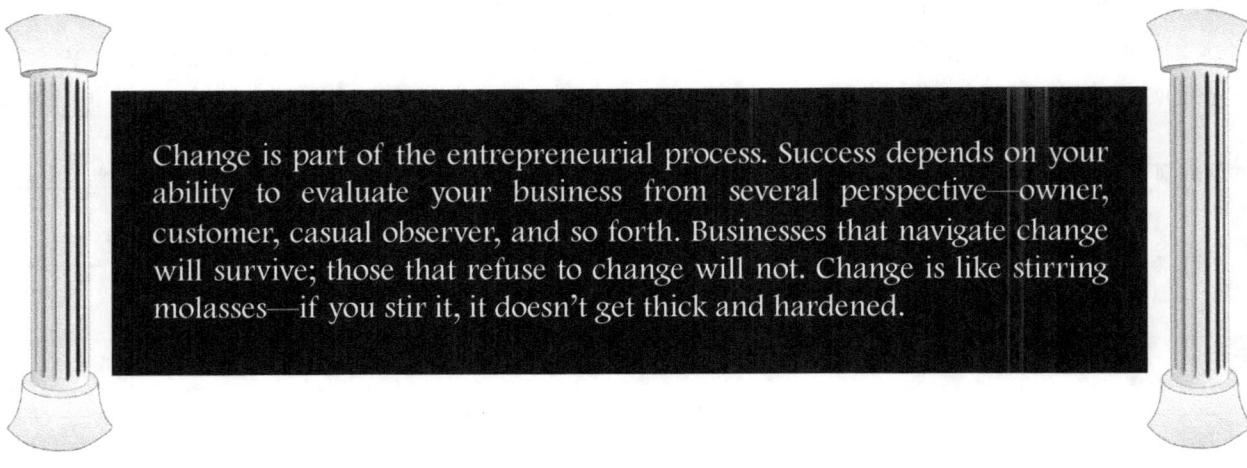

Change is part of the entrepreneurial process. Success depends on your ability to evaluate your business from several perspective—owner, customer, casual observer, and so forth. Businesses that navigate change will survive; those that refuse to change will not. Change is like stirring molasses—if you stir it, it doesn't get thick and hardened.

Start Over Every Year

Each year you need to set aside time to reflect and be deeply critical of your business. In the space below, list your first year goals. _____

_____

_____

_____

_____

_____

At the end of the first year, revisit this list and evaluate your business against the goals you established. Be willing to admit where you fell short and look for ways to improve in the coming year. Also, look closely at goals that were easily attained. Consider adjusting them for the coming year.

After the first year, ask:

• What products or services were not as profitable as anticipated?

• If you could start over, which employees would you NOT hire?

• Which employees are working at their full capacity?

• Which employees need to be challenged or reassigned?

Dream Big, Think Big

What would you do if your business exceeds your expectations? _____

_____

_____

What is your expansion plan? How do you intend to grow the business? _____

_____

_____

Keep A Startup Journal

You will learn a lot during your first year. There will be some mistakes you will never want to repeat. There will be some lessons you never want to forget. The best way to remember is to document what is happening. Writing down your thoughts and actions will be helpful in future business startups and give you fodder for conversations with other entrepreneurs.

> Writing down your thoughts and actions will be helpful in future business startups and give you fodder for conversations with other entrepreneurs.

What is one quote that motivates you to pursue success in business and life? _____

_____

_____

Be inspired every single day. Tell yourself in words and pictures what it is that you are meant to be.

What Happens If You Refuse to Change?

We don't have to think to far back to see evidence of what happens when businesses neglect the need for change. There must be something that separates those companies that survive the test of time from those that simply evaporate from existence.

In our lifetime, we've seen the telephone industry change dramatically. When was the last time you dropped coins into a pay phone? We've seen the entertainment industry totally revamped. You no longer have to stay home to catch your favorite show. You can have anything you want delivered in a short time and never go to a retail store. Change!

List some examples of companies that failed to change and are now either out of business or have lost their position in the marketplace. _____

_____

_____

_____

_____

Identify the changes the following companies failed to make:

Sears _____

_____

Blockbuster Video _____

_____

Circuit City _____

_____

AOL (America On Line) _____

_____

Oldsmobile or Mercury _____

_____

Nokia Cell Phones _____

_____

Montgomery Ward _____

_____

Kmart _____

_____

How can you prevent irrelevance from squeezing the life out of your business? What will you do to maintain or grow your market share? _____

_____

_____

_____

_____

"What If" Is a Good Plan

Let's be honest. All of the research and planning that takes place before a business launch doesn't guarantee its success. If you have everything riding on the back of one product or service, you are taking a giant risk.

> All of the research and planning that takes place before a business launch doesn't guarantee its success.

What other products or services could your company offer if your initial offering doesn't produce the revenue expected? _____

_____

_____

How quickly could you get ready to sell or offer something different? _____

_____

_____

What staffing will you need in order to offer a different product or service? _____

_____

_____

_____

How does the profit margin for the secondary product or service compare to the profit margin of the primary product or service? _____

_____

_____

Who would be your most significant competitors in the secondary product or service market? _____

_____

_____

Describe your competitive advantage related to the secondary product or service. _____

_____

_____

_____

Plan a Staff Retreat

Your perspective is limited. Most leaders think they have a handle on every aspect of their business. They should know more about the business than anyone else, but they don't have the perspectives of their employees. The people who deal with customers see things the leader might never see. The financial expert might see trends the leader easily overlooks. People who work on your website know how visitors are engaging. You need to value the perspectives of those on your team.

One of the best things you can do is plan a staff retreat. That means taking everyone associated with your business to a neutral site where they can let go of their responsibilities and feel like a valuable part of the team. Commit to brainstorming every six months on the following questions:

- What weakness do you presently have in your product or service that a competitor could take advantage of?

- Is there a new technology or way of doing business that could put you out of business if it became more popular?

- Who is your biggest competitor?

- What are they doing that you have to admit is working or effective or noticeable?

- What advertising have you seen by any business that your impressed with and why?

- Is there any way you could duplicate some of these ideas for you business without violating any intellectual property laws of course.

Change will come. You can either learn to leverage it for your benefit or let it overwhelm your business. Many companies have tried to resist change and discovered the futility of that approach. Other companies such as *Apple, Tom's Shoes, Zappos, Amazon*, etc. have been instrumental in introducing change.

How you deal with change will see the stage for your success as an entrepreneur. Choose wisely and choose quickly.